# THE 24/7 HEARTBEAT OF WORSHIP

## Discovering God All the Time, Anywhere

PHYLLIS D. THOMPSON HILLIARD

# DEDICATION

For all the wonders of His mighty hand, during my moments of worship in both solitude and among the throngs of Believers, I dedicate this book right back to God, my greatest inspiration and the Eternal object of my affection.

I love how He has set things in place and in motion throughout the universe, with humanity in mind. And that includes me.

To my beloved Heavenly Father:

THANK YOU.

Happy moments ~ Praise God

Difficult moments ~ Seek God

Quiet moments ~ *WORSHIP GOD*

Painful moments ~ Trust God

Every Moment ~ Thank God

**~ *Anonymous***

Note: When it comes to worship, don't wait until it gets quiet.
You just might miss the moment.

# Preface

In the fall of 2012, I became an online student of Regent School of Divinity in Virginia Beach, Virginia in pursuit of a seminary degree. Two years later in 2014, I took a course with David Edwards, a popular Christian musician and adjunct instructor on the faculty of Regent. The course he taught, *The Worship Leader*, was offered at a very pivotal time in my life: my husband and I had become first-time grandparents on August 29, 2014, just one week after the start of the fall semester.

The syllabus required several reading and writing assignments, as well as discussion board participation. Among the writing, we were required to choose a scripture on worship each week of the semester and expound on it as a journal entry. Also during that week, we had to write a companion *personal* experience on worship.

At this juncture of my life, my worship was at a meteoric high. So very much was grappling for my time, talent, treasure, and attention. I was coerced by personal demands to worship God!

Fast-forward three years later: As I reread my entries, I realized the intensity of my personal worship, the response of God, and the intimacy of my relationship with Him during those fifteen weeks. I wanted and felt compelled to share these experiences.

This book is my offering to God as yet another emblem and expression of worship. It is also my choice to expose to any and all who might be interested in what a semester's worth of one woman's weekly encounters with the Creator of the universe looks like!

Let's sojourn together and worship Yahweh with reckless abandon.

# INTRODUCTION

I never really considered myself a worshipper. I imagined that a worshipper was someone who stood all day, hands uplifted, and a mouth given to continuous prayers. I wouldn't be able to keep up that stance. As much as I admire these women, I'm no Anna the prophetess who's cited in the Gospel of Matthew. Neither am I a disciple of Terèsa of Avila.[1] I just can't bring myself to pray all day long. My early goal in life was to fit the schematics of the virtuous woman whose biography is detailed in Proverbs 31. (Even that sister had to have been exhausted at the end of the day or even sooner!)

Now that time, age, maturity, and circumstances have had their imprint and permanent impact on my life, I have reached a place where I can unequivocally declare myself a worshipper, not just someone who attends church regularly and goes along with the Order of Service.

Let me be clear from the outset: I love God with my entire being. However, I must confess that there have been times when I've neglected to speak to God in prayer, yet wanted Him to move in my behalf. *(Oh, what tangled webs we tend to weave!)* I cannot adequately number the times when I have felt like leaving this whole "Christian walk" and going it my way (whatever that looks like!) Nevertheless, I know where my "help" lies and I know Who loves me without the attachment of conditions. After all this time, where would I go, anyway? I am a dyed-in-the-wool, certified, bona fide, joined-at-the-hip worshipper!

Even as a pastor's wife for 35 years, a preacher for close to that length of time, a credentialed theologian, a student of the Holy Scriptures, a committed Christian, a bold disciple of Jesus, I fall short of the glory of God in several arenas and on many occasions. I feel like an imposter when I delve into worship mode and my heart is loaded with resentment towards someone. So, not only am I a worshipper, I declare that I am a **redeemed sinner still in need of grace**. And in my very costly redemption, I feel freed from guilt, which grants me permission to worship, knowing also that my vulnerability beckons the Divine Cardiologist to readily cleanse and purify my heart…and my motives. He keeps pumping my veins with life-giving blood and infusing my Spirit with His, sanctifying me afresh.

When it comes to overt worship, I am not one who is given to run down the church aisles, nor am I one to erupt in a full-fledged "holy dance." However, you are apt to see me shed tears, my body sway to soft and sometimes muted rhythms, lift my hands, eyes closed in reverence to God. You may even see me kneel in my space to acknowledge the overwhelming glory of His presence. And on a rare occasion, you just may witness me doing a little bit of a "two-step" shuffle with God in church. In the privacy of my home, I may at times lay prostrate on my bedroom floor. It is my method of worship at those moments. He governs my life and I ardently love Him for that. I simply, yet profoundly worship God at any given moment, often without visible expression.

By way of an alternative definition, worship is giving God His due props. My take, also, is that it really doesn't have to be vocal or noisy. Worship can be discreet as well as bodacious.

As I have delved throughout these pages explaining my promptings of worship, I've thought of the phrase usually listed on most Protestant church bulletins in their Order of Service: "Praise and Worship." Nearly every mainline church that operates in the name of Jesus has this rendering at the outset of any service. Throughout the many years of modern church existence, These co-joined twins have come to indicate a 15 to 30-minute (*or more!*) musical preamble to the full congregational experience. The praise team and their songs may often sound and seem like a modified pep rally or concert: *"Come on, everybody! Put your hands together and make some noise!!"* The accompanying hand-clapping and escalating decibels from the appointed Praise Team and musical accompaniment usually brings the audience and congregation to lively participation. On many occasions, it can almost seem rowdy.

Psalm 150 does indeed beckon the believer to "praise Him on the instruments," and so the musicians in the assembly comply. I don't play an instrument, so I use my voice, feet, hands, and most certainly, my heart. That's the praise portion. Admittedly, I have felt gloriously consumed by waves of spirit-filled music, punctuated with the voice of a lead vocalist urging the audience to *"Lift those hands to the Lord." "Put your mind on rewind and think of how far the Lord has brought you." "Close your eyes and think of His goodness."* As the tempo descends, and especially when an old familiar hymn is sung, I involuntarily saunter into the soothing realm of worship.

For me, worship has the audacity to enlarge the possibilities of a God in charge, in spite of what may be glaring evidence to the contrary, that would cause the mightiest of men to bow. As I worship, the Holy Spirit has full reign to minister to my soul, my mind, my circumstances, whereas praise targets and stirs my God-centered emotions. This is so much more than a

Sunday morning experience. From my vantage point, worship is a continuous acknowledgement of God's activity in the earth, coupled with our response to it.

During my years of study towards earning my seminary degree, I upped the ante in my own worship experience. As I began to more closely observe the movement of God in my life and in the earth, it soon became my survival ethos. It is far too easy to become consumed by the pressures and realities heaped upon the frail existence of humans than to abdicate our will and surrender all to God. We may as well submit to the latter, since He has pre-eminence and the capability to handle everything, anyway. Herein, worship becomes an absolute; it becomes imperative. Time and life prove to be the barometers of change everywhere in all things and people. I strongly suggest that the Christian community find ourselves poised and apt to worship at any given moment. Yes, indeed: *pause for the cause!* Yet be ever so vigilant, stay **awake** and **aware** of the pervasive evil lurking and abounding all around.

As you read through the following personal testimonies and the exegesis of the weekly companion scriptures – all dealing with the premise of worship – keep in mind that all these were experienced and written during the winter and spring of 2014 when I was a matriculating seminary student. I've updated many of the details to bring readers current. Secondly, do find yourself as I did, working and walking to reach that point and place where you are forced to surrender and worship round the clock! In many instances, your very life may depend upon this.

*Phyllis Hilliard, author*

# Chapter 1

## <u>IT'S A GRAND AFFAIR</u>

I enjoy being a mother so very much. I believe I literally was born for this. But as of August 29, 2014, God has elevated my position to that of **GRANDmother**! I recall a line in the movie, ***Father of the Bride II*** starring Steve Martin when he finds out his daughter and son-in-law are expecting their first baby. He said, in a bit of a huff, *"Grandparents! What's so grand about it?"*[1]

All these many years later, my answer to that is **"*Are You kidding me*?!! It's EVERYTHING!"**

This sense of euphoria just cannot be accurately described with the few words available in the common dictionary. So allow me to make full expression in this chapter of how this new phase of life has affected me, a woman who, as a little girl, couldn't wait to get married and be a mother. And now…***this!*** Talk about worship!!! Mine went through the roof! Among so much else, my grandson's birth was and remains a touchstone occasion of worship for me.

These days, I'm feeling rather grand…like a piano, a ballroom, an entrance! Carpe diem!

# <u>AUGUST 20</u>

As I rubbed our youngest daughter's big, round belly and sang to our grandson still growing within the safe confines of her womb, he responded to me with various movements. Her belly became misshapen with the turning of what could be his foot, buttocks, hand, or perhaps his elbow! Is he chiming in with his grandmother's voice? Is this outside stimuli disturbing his rest? Was the baby's movement *his* moment of worship?

What is for certain was my amazement at God's gift of life. I began to worship knowing that within two weeks, I will be holding new life, presenting yet another generation of our family and the evidence of God's proclamation of life. Hallelujah! I'm so excited!! God be praised!!

To most grandparents, this is an opportunity to right a few wrongs they may have felt were unconsciously (or intentionally) done to their children. Becoming a grandparent- as I have been told through the years - was that they should have been grandparents FIRST, then had children. I've also been told how you can spoil and enjoy grandchildren, then send them right back home. My favorite anecdote that I used to hear is that having grandchildren can sometimes disguise itself as sweet revenge on your children.

Whatever the case, I tucked all these quips and tips in my mind until now. My husband and I will soon be on that proverbial stage with an innumerable host of others, touting our new status as grandparents. I'm here to report that WE CANNOT WAIT!!

*(Photo: personal collection of Phyllis Hilliard)*

# <u>AUGUST 29</u>

It is in the wee hours of Friday morning and my youngest daughter is about to have her first baby. Her husband stood by her hospital bed, holding her legs, and the nurse instructed our daughter to push. It wasn't long before our first grandchild, Joseph Donald, emerged from her loins. It was a bloody, messy process, yet filled with so much wonder!!!

I began to cry and shake as I saw my daughter agonizing as she pushed with all her might to deliver her son. I fell to my knees and I worshipped God for the gift of life. We were jubilant at his arrival and amazed when we saw this beautiful little boy open his eyes, release a tiny inaugural cry, and then…nothing. Suddenly, as the OB doctor began to place this fresh new bundle of life onto my daughter's bosom - skin to skin, at her request - we were told to stand back. Then the doctor called for the head nurse from the NICU and the Emergency Response team. As he then lay in the plastic crib, I noticed Joseph now had a blank stare, unaccompanied by familiar newborn infant cries. The NICU head nurse began to shake his face rather vigorously to "stimulate" him, she said. His heart rate – which was SO strong and vibrant in vitro – was now dropping.

Initially, I panicked when I saw all the commotion around our new gift. Then… I thought of Job – who, according to scripture, had lost all ten of his children when their house was destroyed as a result of a horrific tornado.[2] I thought also of King David, when he and Bathsheba lost their infant child. Unfortunately, in King David's case, this child was the result of his adulterous behavior and Bathsheba's reluctant submission to the wanton appetite of the nation's ruler.[3] Nevertheless, the loss of this child was a painful, searing nightmare. Within one year, Bathsheba lost her husband, Uriah, and her firstborn child, which was illicitly sired by the King of Jerusalem.

In either of these accounts, both Job and King David resorted to worshiping God upon hearing the news of the death of their offspring. Bearing this in mind and simultaneously rebuking death with fervent prayer, I, too, began to worship, despite what by all appearances seemed ever so grim. On my knees, already in a posture of prayer, I began to audibly and relentlessly wail and pray.

When I resumed my composure many minutes later, my husband told me that one of the medics had placed an oxygen mask on Joseph's tiny face. Although I missed seeing this since I was already on my knees with my back turned towards this frantic post-natal mission, it was all too clear that our baby was in serious trouble. So dire was Joseph's condition, our daughter refused to look towards her baby, fearing that she could possibly go home empty-handed. Ah, but the intervening power of prayer and of worship prevailed in that delivery room!!

Praise report: Joseph Donald has survived and is thriving! I remain in worship mode and give all praise to our God for sustaining the life of our precious grandson. I am fully aware that every diabolical agent, imp, and demon in hell would have been greatly satisfied to have had things go differently.

The ultimate and indisputable verdict: **GOD reigns**…and He is *SO* good. I cannot help but worship Him. I owe God that much.

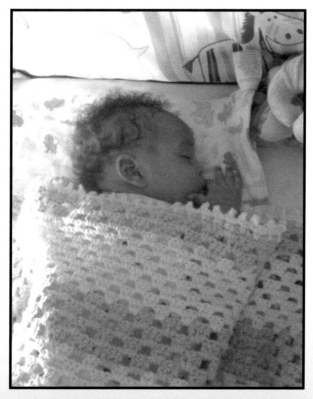

*(Photo: personal collection of Phyllis Hilliard)*

# **<u>SEPTEMBER 20</u>**

For the past three weeks, I have been living with our youngest daughter and her husband after she gave birth to their first child together on August 29th. It has been my great honor and privilege to do their food shopping, to purchase new bedding for them, to cook their meals, to wash dishes and laundry, to clean their home, and to assist with caring for their newborn son, our very first grandchild!!

My son-in-love's mother and sister came with the same agenda three weeks later. I am now going to share this great pleasure with them and take my leave. All the while I was in my daughter's home, I thanked and worshiped God that they were even able to purchase and maintain their own place.

On my way down the highway driving alone, I worshipped God in that our daughter is being cared for by a gentleman who adores her. I worshipped God that she has the same opportunity and great privilege as I to be a mother and to shape a life. At the remembrance of baby Joseph's struggle to survive immediately after birth, I worshipped God that he is a thriving little bundle of absolute joy.

I worship God that I am in excellent health and can "do" for my family. I take NOTHING for granted.

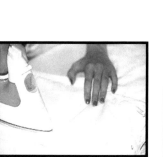
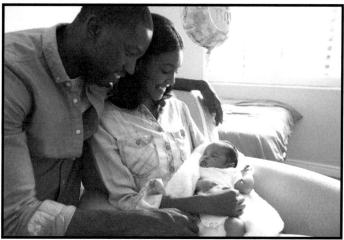

*(All photos: Thinkstock.com)*

# NOVEMBER 16

The birth of our first grandchild has irrevocably altered my life. I've committed to caring for him while his parents work, to save on childcare expenses, to avoid having strangers look after him, and to prevent exposure to the predictably frigid elements. However, they live in Maryland; we live in New Jersey.

My act of worship to God for sparing my grandson's life at birth is to drive down each week in all kinds of weather to care for him, then drive back to New Jersey on the weekend to see about my husband and to fulfill my pastoral duties at our satellite church. I then drive back down on Sunday or very early Monday morning to start all over again.

I worship continuously during the nearly three-hour, 159-mile trek (one way) coming and going. It is my offering both to God and to my children. This is my assignment and the assignment is my worship. It is my ode of gratitude to God for what is owed.

*(Photo: personal collection of Phyllis Hilliard)*

# Chapter 2

## <u>MATING SEASON</u>

*"And the Lord God said, "It is not good that man should be alone.*
*I will make him a helper comparable to him." ~ Genesis 2:18*

At this writing, it has been a 37-year journey. September 12, 1981 witnessed a young woman who had just turned 22 years old a mere five days earlier, say "I do" to a slender 24-year old, handsome dynamo of a preacher. We had dated for a year before Donald asked me to be his wife – December 30, 1980 in his parents' basement - to be exact. I was elated, shocked, dazzled, and went running upstairs to show his folks what they had already seen and known about – my engagement ring.

As I worshipped in church each Sunday thereafter, I was sure to raise my left hand in adoration to God for His great blessings—and for any spectators to see the new glimmer not only in my eyes, but on my left ring finger!

Over these more than three and a half decades of marriage, I can attest that our tight-knit relationship with God has been our mutual anchor, keeping us afloat amid turbulent waters that have often beset our lives, particularly in ministry. Oh yes, despite the celebrity, occasional perks, and the "lights, camera, action" components, ministry is an extremely demanding vocation. The weight of it can invariably creep into any unsuspecting relationship and wreak all kinds of havoc. I am convinced that our determination to make a steady path to God's door, to worship, and press through rising muddy waters has been our saving grace. We've nearly drowned as our "love boat" has frequently capsized. But, we're still here…another season, donning our life jackets, using our oars of grace and mercy to row with or against certain tides, doing our best to stay buoyant and intact as Mr. and Mrs.

September 12, 1981                    December 2014

*(Photos: personal collection of Phyllis Hilliard)*

# SEPTEMBER 12

Today, my husband and I celebrated our thirty-third wedding anniversary. As I mulled over the whirlwind activity of the past year and stretched my memory to the innumerable triumphs, trials, victories, good times, mishaps, and misunderstandings over the past three *decades*, I had to conclude that *"God is our refuge and strength, a very present help in the time of trouble."*
   *(Psalm 46:1)*

   We have had the lion's share of marital missteps, of wanting to throw in the proverbial towel, quit the ministry (I felt this, anyway) AND EACH OTHER and be relieved of endless demands and obligations. However, at the end of the day and when all is said and done, marriage is God's way of championing His cause for remaining in a committed relationship with Him. This is His noble reflection of a Christian's determination and responsibility to "tough it out" and remain connected and "married" to Him, even when our prayers seem to be muted by the cacophony of life and God's deafening silence.

   For the past two and half weeks, and for the remainder of our lives, our marriage has taken on another life chapter, in that we have joined the ranks of an elite populace: ***grandparents.***

   I thank God, I worship God for the opportunity to help shape another generation. I worship God for giving us the fortitude to carry on in marriage, particularly as front line, public people. It ain't easy, but it is just what it is.

*(Photo source: Thinkstock.com)*

# <u>OCTOBER 5</u>

My husband and I rose before dawn to be at the airport in time for our 7:45 a.m. flight to Cancun, Mexico. After a 2-legged journey totaling five long hours in the air (*the last two were spent crammed in the very last seats on the plane. No reclining or stretching for us!),* we finally landed in this beautiful country. Weary yet relieved, I found myself reflecting on the many news reports of hijackings, explosions, and crashes of international as well as domestic flights over the past year.

    Each time any of us boards a subway, bus, train, plane, or even our cars, it is God who grants us safe passage to our destinations. While we were airborne and certainly upon deplaning, I found myself pulling my suitcase and silently worshipping God for once again keeping us safe and alive.

    Much credit is due and given to pilots for their aviation skill and navigational acuity. By all means, they do deserve recognition. But I am aware of the real deal, and from me, God gets the loudest and most abundant accolades!! On a more selfish note: it felt SO GOOD to get away and enjoy one another without interruption or obligations.

*(Photo source: Thinkstock.com)*

# <u>OCTOBER 13</u>

Although this week is designated as our fall semester break at Regent University, there is no suspension of time in worshipping GOD; it is continual and always befitting. Throughout the past eight days, my husband and I have enjoyed vacationing in Cancun, Mexico. We have dined, we have laid on the white sandy beach, we have walked downtown and perused some of the shops, we have listened to a Mexican male trio perform at one of the restaurants, playing their guitars and singing songs indigenous to their homeland and in honor of our 33rd wedding anniversary. We have been blessed beyond appropriate words and measure. I have lugged my laptop, books, and assignments with me along these thousands of miles. I have interrupted time with my husband to upload assignments and, as I put it, "try to stay on top of my academic game."

Each day, I found myself going out onto the balcony of our hotel room and gazing at the breathtaking Gulf of Mexico with its graduated shades of aqua and turquoise, seagulls flying overhead. I just had to worship God each and every day for His creation. I am fully aware that all of Mexico is not so grand and glorious, not so peaceful, not so inviting. However, from this vantage point, I am compelled and MUST worship God for His indescribable handiwork.

My husband and I will take our leave of this 5-diamond kingdom on tomorrow and head back to New Jersey, USA where our lives of ministry and non-stop obligations await us. But It is not without an intentional effort of worshipping the God Who has called and equipped us as a couple to serve Him and His people. We leave with worship-filled hearts knowing that God is at the helm of our lives. I leave this place feeling engulfed by God, in every sinew of my being. I daily worshipped God while visiting this foreign land…just because of Who He is.

*(Photo: personal collection of Phyllis Hilliard)*

# Chapter 3

# <u>NATURE'S CALL</u>

*"As long as the earth endures, seedtime and harvest, cold and heat, summer and winter, day and night, will never cease." (Genesis 8:22)*

Growing up in Elizabeth, New Jersey, I loved the fall season, particularly the beginning of a new school year. *(Yes, I was the quintessential grammar school geek!)* What intrigued me most about this time of year was this giant tree on our street. Every autumn, the sidewalk would be littered with these round, green prickly things. When the green 'things' that managed to hang on finally came into full bloom, They cracked open and spilled out brown chestnuts all over the sidewalk. Little did any of us know or care at that time that we had access to some costly nuts, much less trees lining an inner-city sidewalk.

As autumn gave way to winter, these same trees that formerly were filled with some strange green object dangling from their branches, soon began to litter these same sidewalks even more, along with their brown, withered crunchy leaves. Only this time, they,  too, had turned brown. Along with soft twigs that had also fallen, they all crunched under our feet as we walked to school. Those round green, prickly things that grew so abundantly on that enormous tree had become dry, discolored easily cracking open and revealing either the  misshapen, shrunken, dead chestnut treasure inside…or nothing.

It has always amazed me how seasons take on a personality of their own for a certain amount of time. God has awesomely designed seasons with a built-in timer, instructing them when and where to bud, to ripen, to produce, to shed, to cease, and when to start this process all over again. It is undeniable – although many have tried – that all of this activity and more are covertly ordained by God. One season closes, another gets a curtain call to begin a fresh act in nature's show.

Our lives often take on the same attributes as nature. We embark on certain activities that ultimately encompass a "season" in our lives. Then, either we lose interest and opt out. Or "life happens." Or, there is a shift towards yet another season. Some seasons are quite profitable, even joyful; others, not so much. The wiser choice is not to quit, but rather adjust to the eminent change at hand. After all, isn't that the one constant in life: CHANGE? God made this clear to us in the book of Genesis. This being written and said, I've learned to embrace, appreciate, and revel in each season, …eventually. Just like nature, flexibility and change are a part of my calling. I won't fudge the truth and say that I like and enjoy every season thrust upon me or even those I've chosen.

Nevertheless, when God calls and the seasons change, I want to avail myself and respond with a heart leaning in to worship, no matter what. I might as well. After all, God told us in advance that the seasons would never cease. I can just about hear Nature say, as the late boxing champion Muhammad Ali once told the world, "…*get used to me!*"[1]

# SEPTEMBER 6

Suddenly this afternoon, the skies unleashed an unrelenting descent of rain accompanied by the menacing sound of claps of thunder. For the previous few weeks, the atmosphere had been enduring scorching heat, with little signs of relief…until now. For me, this was indeed a moment of worship, as I looked out the front window of my daughter's home and thought of the scripture where rain *"waters the earth… to give seed to the sower and bread to the eater" (Isaiah 55:10)*. Everything in this life has been ordained by God and serves a purpose, regardless as to how discomforting or satisfying it may be.

The rain has cleansed portions of the earth. The rain has been an answer to the prayers of many farmers who suspected and perhaps feared a drought. The rain has given life to withering plants and foliage. The rain has brought the temperature to a bearable degree for us miserable mortals.

I paused for the cause and gave God a great applause…for the rain. As I turn fifty-five years young on tomorrow, I have asked God to "rain" down unparalleled and immeasurable favor upon me, as well. And so, I shall worship Him…in advance…whether favor appears to be evident or not. And you know, sometimes change is good for what ails us.

*(Photo source: Thinkstock.com)*

# <u>OCTOBER 21</u>

Just before the "official" calendar advent of autumn, the leaves began their annual transformation of color. This is a typical occurrence of the seasons' change; it's nothing new. But for some reason, the majesty of it all really struck me this year as I drove down the quiet road which leads to our home. The township-appointed trees were so very stunning in their varying shades of gold, celadon, burnt orange, crimson, and sienna, among a few evergreens.

I focused keenly on these colors, recalling the uniformed greens they were clothed in only weeks earlier. Each leaf had been summoned by God to change their garment to welcome and embrace a fresh season. I found myself bedazzled by the unsurpassed beauty of this foliage. Suddenly, I segued into a posture of worship as I recognized the handiwork of the Divine Painter of this mesmerizing landscape. What came to me was the old hymn, **How Great Thou Art**. In particular, I thought of the verse which says,

> *"O Lord, my God, when I, in awesome wonder, consider*
> *all the works Thy hands have made. I see the stars, I hear*
> *the roaring thunder, Thy power throughout the universe displayed."*[2]

*(Photo: personal collection of Phyllis Hilliard)*

# Chapter 4

# <u>RADICAL SABBATICAL</u>

**sab•bat•i•cal:**[1] *(noun)*
*1) of or pertaining to or appropriate to the Sabbath*
*2) bringing a period of rest*
*3) any extended period of leave from one's customary work*

Jesus addressed Sabbath rest with His disciples in the Gospel according to Mark when He instructed them to *"come aside and rest awhile."*[2] Why is it that we humans work, run, do, REPEAT, and make little time for ample rest? When do we just ponder and wonder? And for the Christian, when do we literally and fully acknowledge the directive of Moses when he told the Israelites to *"stand still and see the salvation of the Lord?" (Exodus14:13),* just for a fleeting moment?

Who is it we're yearning to impress or satisfy with these unreasonable schedules? Pleasing the boss at any cost? Suffering from the 'disease to please'? Breaking glass ceilings with skill and tenacity (or a mallet)? Fulfilling our personal and endless agendas? No matter the reach, the influence, or the reward of the climb, we frail humans still need to disconnect, recharge, refresh, and… *come aside.* Let's not forget that God had already established the proper template for work and rest, as recorded in Genesis chapter 2, verse 1.

Now here's our narrative:

My husband has worked tirelessly pastoring our church for over thirty-five years. His efforts and imprint could be seen and felt around the city where our church is located. For example, years ago when we painted our properties a beautiful pale purple, several neighboring businesses immediately followed suit! My husband has been a trendsetter for many years, a take-charge go-getter, unafraid to take risks and believe God for fulfillment and advancement. Our church has been blessed to open a restaurant, a floral shop, a school, an after-school program, a summer camp, and so much more. We now have tenants occupying a few of our properties. For the first two and half decades of serving as Senior Pastor, my husband ran hard. Ridiculously hard. Donald Hilliard, Jr. was relentless in his pursuit of ministry and fulfilling the call of God on his life.

He was a young, trailblazing maverick, full of energy, determined to fulfill God's will for our local assembly. The problem is that as the years rolled by, he rarely slowed down. As he's gotten older, it began to catch up with him, to the point of compromising his health. In 2005, he had major surgery on his colon. In 2006, he was dealing with a cardiac condition. In 2012, he contracted a life-threatening virus. Then in 2013, he lost his mother, with whom he was very, very close. During this new and dreadful life chapter, it became more and more apparent that Bishop Hilliard needed to rest for an extended time. Stress was mounting, depression was calling, and burnout was imminent. Yet, my husband kept preaching hard, traveling, being a true pastor to his congregation. This is a formula for certain disaster. Wayne Cordeiro, author of *Leading on Empty*, put it like this:

> *"Long term stress is a predecessor to depression. The constant expectation to come up with yet another inspiring message wears you out. It depletes our emotional system, reducing your ability to stay balanced. Long-term stress is not detectable in the beginning. It is well disguised by growing success, financial prosperity, or people's accolades. The numbing effect keeps you pressing forward, leading on empty, until the bottom falls out. Then success is no longer your goal. Healing is."*[3]

My husband was at a critical emotional, psychological, physiological, and pastoral crossroads, for sure. So, after a few noble attempts over a number of years applying for a much-needed, long-overdue sabbatical, the extensive efforts finally came to fruition in August 2014! Our church would be sending my husband on a three-month sabbatical. (Of course, when- and wherever he traveled, I would come along, too).

For two solid weeks during this time, my husband went for extensive physical, emotional, and mental examinations to a faraway, unfamiliar place. This is the true purpose of Sabbath rest: to be led to still waters and have one's soul restored *(Psalm 23:2)*. Lord knows, he desperately needed that. He spent time writing. He also worked on an academic project with a colleague who is an adjunct seminary professor.

For us, this was quite a radical experience – being out of the whole church rhythm for this long stretch of time. It's one thing to be on vacation for a few weeks; it's quite another to be absent from your source of duty (and income) for an entire quarter. There's more truth than a little bit to the old adage, "out of sight, out of mind." When the set man or woman of a religious institution, or any other organization is absent for an extended length of time, people are apt to begin looking elsewhere to satiate their spiritual or otherwise appetite. I began to wonder if that would become our lot, after having put in SO MUCH effort, sweat, resources, tears and years? Thoughts of congregational loyalty and financial stability were of concern. Would we recognize our church when we returned? Would my husband's three decades of labor be honored, neglected, or Worse…forgotten? Call me paranoid, but a whole lot can happen within a three-month period…*anywhere.*

Certainly, our church boasts of an awesome team of administrative and pastoral leaders, overseeing the managerial tedium that comes with a high-octane ministry, and carrying the weight of the magnanimous enterprise known as Cathedral International. Nevertheless, varying thoughts of what would be facing us upon our return still ran through my mind.

Finally and with much anticipated relief, we fully trusted and are here to report even four years later, that all was, is, and remains well and intact. Let the church roll on.

# <u>OCTOBER 1</u>

I accompanied my husband to a church in Queens Village, New York, where he was scheduled to speak for their church's anniversary service. The choir sang hymns and the atmosphere was primed for worship. I sat there weeping, lifting my hands, swaying to the familiar melodic tunes and lyrics of *"Great is Thy Faithfulness,"* and *"How Firm a Foundation."* This was an exclusive and intense moment of worship for me. It had been a while since I have occupied this space.

It was rather surreal in that church attendance has been irregular for us during this three-month sabbatical. At this moment in time, I was immersed in worship. I felt consumed, as though God had cloaked and swaddled me with a restorative measure of His grace.

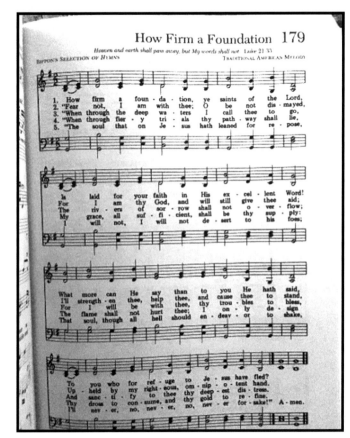

*(Photos: personal collection of Phyllis Hilliard)*

# <u>NOVEMBER 2</u>

For the past three months, my husband has been away from our church for a well-deserved, first-time-in-thirty-one-years' sabbatical. Today is our first Sunday back; it is Communion Sunday. As we stood side by side at the high altar in our sanctuary, my husband recited the words of the Apostle Paul to the Corinthian church concerning the body and the blood of Jesus. Our musician began to softly play an old hymn, *"Oh, How He Loves You and Me."* My mind drifted to a place far from where I actually stood.

I felt cradled by God at that very moment when I recognized the melody. Aware of my clerical duties and surroundings, lights and cameras accosting us in front, and the choir behind us, I silently worshipped God, grateful for His stubborn and inclusive love.

It had been years since I'd heard that old hymn, yet it evoked an impassioned yearning within me for the *'more'* of God. I felt compelled to worship. During Communion, I had to subdue my desire to really *"get into the moment"* and *"go in"* as I stood at the sacred table before the congregation. So I settled for quiet tears.

*(Photo source: Thinkstock.com)*

# __NOVEMBER 9__

Since my husband has been on sabbatical for the past three months, he and I have been absent from the life of any of the three churches under the Cathedral International banner. As of January 2013, I have been stationed as a preaching Staff Pastor at our satellite church in Asbury Park, 40 minutes from our base location in Perth Amboy where we returned November 2nd.

I returned to Asbury Park today, Sunday, November 9th in my capacity as a preacher. Having acclimated to the much smaller setting of this locale as compared to our very large main campus, I have grown very fond of this church and its congregants, just as I have to those who attend our services in Perth Amboy. It felt SO very good to be back with them! I worshipped God in my spirit and overtly when I mounted the pulpit to give warm greetings and then to deliver my sermon.

It is my pleasure to serve these people and wherever else I am assigned. I give God thanks for them, leading me to a place of worship, and for the privilege that is mine to be among them once again after such an extended leave of absence. I worshipped God when a woman testified about her lengthy drug addiction and her hard-won deliverance, sealing her testimony with a song. I worshipped as I looked out among the sparsely attended congregation, a witness to its very slow, but evident growth. I worshipped God when the praise team had added three male voices to its ranks!

While it may seem trite and insignificant to most people, these were signs to me that God intends for His church to remain, to grow, and to ultimately thrive.

*...and the gates of Hades shall **NOT** prevail against it. ~ Matthew 16:18*

*(Photo: personal collection of Phyllis Hilliard)*

# Chapter 5

# <u>HUMILITY</u>

**hōō • mil´• i• tē**
*1) the quality or condition of being humble;*
*2) modest opinion or estimate of one's own importance*

When I think of this word, what comes to mind are various occasions where and when I perhaps made an unfair judgment and the evidence at hand proved me wrong. That was humbling. Whether it was an unflattering display gone public or my attempt to bless someone without others knowing, humility is that attribute that doesn't mind the anonymity of the shadows. I am not comfortable with public accolades, preferring the spotlight to be elsewhere. I don't feel it is always necessary to celebrate each and every good deed done all the time. After all, didn't Jesus advise us to *"not let the left hand know what the right hand is doing"?*[2] Shouldn't we all just consider ourselves favored and fortunate to be able to render random acts of kindness?

Let's not get this twisted: humility is not to be mistaken for humiliation. Humiliation is the act or feeling of brute embarrassment. Webster's dictionary defines it as: *mortification.*[3] Ouch! Ever been there, when you feel like you could just die right on the spot?

It is to our advantage to practice humility and not have it shoved in our face, having to "eat humble pie." That's no compliment; this phrase clearly implicates one as having been knocked off a pedestal or high-horse and brought to a lower plane, as in ***"Eat your own words!"*** Now **THAT'S** humiliation! I'd rather take the road that leads to humility any day.

I am humbled when an elder person seeks *my* counsel. I am humbled when a beautiful woman bothers to notice and compliment *me* on how 'together' and lovely I may look. I am humbled that God still sends *me* places and uses me to defend His great Gospel. I am humbled that God selected *me* to be the mother of three amazing daughters and the grandmother of a charming grandson.

The following entries are cases of humility, brought on by the Master Architect of life, Himself. In each scenario, the crowning point which led to and sustained the moments of humility was, in effect, worship.

# <u>SEPTEMBER 24</u>

I visited an older friend of mine who very recently lost a second daughter to cancer. When she joined me on her living room sofa after finishing a phone call; she insisted on resting **my** feet on her lap. She is older than my own mother would have been had Mommy lived, yet this woman desired to "serve" me. I couldn't help but envision how it must have been for Jesus – as recorded in the Gospel of Luke - when an anonymous woman broke an alabaster box of costly fragrant oil, anointed his feet, and wiped the dripping excess with her hair.[4] This was a humbling act indeed, as was this moment for me with my friend.

Gram-Gram, as she is affectionately called, began to gently rub my feet, as we sat and talked for what became more than an hour. In an uncanny way, it was as if this were her way of worshipping God in her own secretive manner. We spoke of her having lost three children over the past few years. When I asked how she had endured these tragedies, she explained that she had not "buried" three children, but that they were living in Heaven with Jesus, awaiting her arrival.

Tears streamed down my face as I listened to what to me did not seem sensible or rational. I was left to not only admire this woman's indomitable courage, but I was forced to worship God, literally in spirit and in truth…even in opposition to my aching breaking heart in *her* behalf.

*(Photo source: Thinkstock.com)*

# OCTOBER 29

My husband and I have done a great deal of travelling over the past couple of months. I normally handle our grocery shopping and as a result, the pantry, cabinets, and refrigerator are well-stocked. The family's plates and palates are always satisfied. Unfortunately, when we finally did land back at home, there was absolutely nothing there to eat. We had consumed what was there prior to our three-month sabbatical, which merged with our new life as grandparents.

I scoured the cupboards and refrigerator for something – *ANYTHING!* –to make a meal; I was really hungry. Suddenly, my homespun, "make do" intellect kicked in. I took out an onion, sliced and seasoned it, then grilled it on the stove. I spotted a can of turkey gravy in the pantry. There was one slice of bread left in the fridge! Put it all together and whaddaya have?

By the grace of God, we live a very comfortable life and want for nothing. But this day, we were faced with a defining moment when plenty appeared to have worn the mask of lack. None of this changed Who God is. Believe it or don't: this was a moment of pure worship for me. My meal – if you can call it so - was nowhere near ample, nor filling, for that matter. Minimal though it was, however, Jehovah Jireh[5] had provided, as He did for Abraham in Genesis 22:7.

May I also confess that this experience elicited two responses from me: First, I laughed and then… I *worshipped.* To quote and concur with the ancient psalmist, *"I have been young and now I am old, yet I've never seen the righteous forsaken nor His seed begging bread" (Psalm 37:25).* Even when I cannot trace God's hand, I can always trust His heart. He is not a deadbeat dad. He will never neglect His children, by any means. He is God Almighty and will always provide for His children. That alone obligates me to worship.

*(Photo: personal collection of Phyllis Hilliard)*

# NOVEMBER 23

The demonstration and aroma of worship filled our sanctuary this morning! The church is celebrating my husband's 31st pastoral anniversary. When we came to this inner city congregation in 1983, we never fathomed that God would erupt that 125-member church, causing exponential growth into the thousands, and grant us international exposure, White House invitations, and a very comfortable lifestyle. We sought to be faithful servants, preach the word, and love God's people with a genuine heart. My husband has preached across this country, in foreign lands, and in prestigious settings, such as a Roundtable at Oxford University in London, England. We have had our season on television, radio, and in print. We have been favored with having celebrities from academia, film, music, politics, sports, and other sectors attend our services and even grace the pulpit of our church. The Cathedral International family and the Hilliard's have been immeasurably blessed.

On this anniversary Sunday, the guest preachers for both services echoed loving and lofty sentiments as they stood to deliver their messages. These platitudes caused my husband and me to reflect on and recall the faithfulness of Almighty God over these three decades of pastoral ministry. All of this was so very humbling.

I sat on the pulpit and worshipped God in spirit and in truth at the thought that He would dare bother extending such great favor to us. It brought me to the point of inquiring of God as the psalmist had done over two millennia ago: *"What shall I render unto God for His benefits toward me?"* (Psalm 116:12).

My answer is that *I SHALL UNCEASINGLY **WORSHIP**!*

*(Photo courtesy: personal collection of Phyllis Hilliard)*

# JUST WHAT *IS* WORSHIP?

*wûr´• ship (noun, verb)*
*1) adoration, homage, etc. given to a deity.*
*2) the rituals, prayers, etc. expressing such adoration or homage.*
*3) excessive or ardent admiration or love.*
*4) the object of such love or admiration.*

Just like love, worship is both noun *(an act)* and verb *(it's what you do)*. As a matter of fact, the act of worship as recorded throughout the Holy Scriptures, is seen as loving and having intimate communion with God. From incense and burnt offerings on the ancient Biblical altars, to  contemplative posture today, worship takes the Christian believer to a place of holy reckoning with the Highest Authority, the One who is extolled as Yahweh, Jehovah, the Creator of the universe, El Shaddai, Alpha and Omega, God Almighty, or as some casually refer to as, "the man upstairs."

The following fifteen entries are my take on specifically selected scriptures revolving around the offering of excessive adoration to God. Throughout the examples mined from both the Old and New Testaments, we will see where, when, why, and who made a defining or impromptu decision to worship Jesus and His Father. The divinity course, *"The Worship Leader,"* of which this book was spawned, has prompted me to further investigate this practice of 'ardent admiration.'

I am convinced by virtue of my personal experience as a Christian for over forty years, that the exercise of worship most inclines the heart of God to 'move the needle,' as it were, in our lives. This is not to say that when we want or need a particular thing, we ought to go into robot-mode: stop, worship, and wait for the Heavens to descend a favor. Personally speaking, my walk with God has proven that it doesn't quite work that way. ***"No"*** and/or ***"wait"*** has often been His response to certain requests.

Worship, my beloved audience, is a dish best served raw and constant, twenty-four hours a day, seven days a week. I learned this long before matriculating at Regent University ever crossed my mind.

So, let's get on with the business of adoring and loving God just for Who He is, and rehearsing His flawless and extraordinary resume, which prompted generations of our forebears to worship…anticipating nothing in return. They set the template. Now let's raise the bar.

# <u>WEEK 1</u>

### From the Scriptures

*When he saw Jesus from afar, he ran and worshipped Him. ~ Mark 5:6*

This particular verse tells of a demon-possessed man who recognized the deity of Jesus at a distance. His response to a mere gaze at Jesus was to run towards Him and engage in an act of worship. The scripture is not clear as to how this was expressed. Did he bow? Did he grab the ankles and kiss the feet of Jesus? Did he embrace Him? Did this demoniac lift his hands and sing or recite a psalm?

My take is that this man – riddled with demons – had the presence of mind to bow down in humble submission to a God-sent man whom he was meeting for the first time, and then worship Him. No music ministry, no compelling testimonies… just pure, raw, immediate, uninhibited worship.

*(Sketch source: lavistachurchofchrist.org)*

# <u>WEEK 2</u>

### From the Scriptures

*Then Job arose, tore his robe, and shaved his head, and he*
*fell to the ground and worshipped. ~Job 1:20*

What manner of man was Job, that he could offer himself to God in worship after hearing and enduring such devastation? He had been affected economically, personally, socially, physically, and emotionally… yet without complaint. And to think, there was more to come!!

I have often wondered if I could handle a barrage of bad news and events invading my life concurrently, as nobly as Job did. Would worship even dawn on me as a response to tumultuous tidings, one incident right after the other? Am I that "tight" with God that whatever He allows to come my way, my response would be to worship and not be angered nor repulsed by the dictates of His hand?

*(Sketches: lavistachurchofchrist.org)*

# WEEK 3

### From the Scriptures

*"Give to the Lord the glory due His name; bring an offering and come before Him.*
*Oh, worship the Lord in the beauty of holiness." ~ 1 Chronicles 16:29*

This mention of worship is somewhat of a charge nestled in King David's lengthy song of thanksgiving to God after the ark was brought to Jerusalem. David gives a four-fold directive to his rapt audience: G**ive, bring, come**, and **worship**. As I see it, each of these directives is a form of worship. Giving God glory, rendering an offering, coming into His presence, and availing oneself to be bathed in holiness. They are all such meaningful and extraordinary examples of worship.

I am especially struck by David's exclamatory prefix where he says, "***Oh.***" In my estimation, this reflects his own awe and immeasurable gratitude to God for His great mercy and unmerited favor.

**Praise leads to worship.**

**Giving IS worship.**

*(Photos: Thinkstock.com)*

# WEEK 4

**From the scriptures**

*"Give to the Lord the glory due His name; worship the Lord
in the beauty of holiness." ~ Psalm 29:2*

The first portion of this verse reminds me that I am literally indebted to God, "...*the glory **due** His name.*" The currency at this point is simply worship.

Then the psalmist completes his recommendation by telling us all to worship God, not just as a space filler, but because it is an exercise in total abandonment. He gives a soft command for people to purposefully neglect any and all insignificant attachments, encumbrances, and weight, thus enabling a pure and holy rendering of worship.

*(Photo source: Thinkstock.com)*

# WEEK 5

**From the scriptures**

*"And they worshipped Him, and returned to Jerusalem with great joy."*
~ *Luke 24:52*

This passage of scripture from Luke's Gospel records what occurred *after* the Resurrection of Jesus. He had not only come back to life, but had surreptitiously walked with them through Emmaus and as far as Bethany as they recounted the recent events, which were abuzz throughout the region. He listened to their accounts, walked with them, broke bread with them and when they finally got over their fright and recognized who the resurrected Jesus was, He gave them instructions to go back and wait in Jerusalem for the fulfillment of His promise, which was the coming of the Holy Spirit (Acts 2:1-4).

I can only imagine the ecstatic fervor that must have overtaken the disciples at that moment, to the point where all they could do was worship the living Christ as He took His leave. Others had worshipped Jesus during His tenure as an itinerant preacher, teacher, and healer of all diseases, and for His great miracles. Now, the remaining eleven men (*Judas committed suicide after betraying Jesus*) who had been his closest companions for nearly three years, took the time to absorb the spectacular events that had taken place over the weekend and now, they too, worshipped Jesus.

*(Photo source: Thinkstock.com)*

# <u>WEEK 6</u>

### From the Scriptures

*"And Abraham said to his young men, 'Abide here with the mule while I and my son go yonder and worship, and come again to you.'"* ~ Genesis 22:5

Abraham knew well of his assignment from God to sacrifice his son, Isaac, that very day. However, I believe that in the very depths of his soul, he agonized over this ensuing act of obedience and spoke instead to his assistants of his "intention" to go worship God, with his young son in tow. How often have we set out for a task given to us by God that we absolutely dreaded, but in obedience to Him, forged ahead? Our compliance, in many instances, has prompted God to relent, reverse, and dismiss His own command.

The ram caught in the thicket saved the day for both Isaac and his father, Abraham. In the heat of the moment, God will surely send a ram in the bush for those who have said "yes." Do know that "yes" is not a futile answer. It is a passageway to the heart of God, ushering us into the holy of holies, the most intimate arena of where God dwells.

*(Sketch source: lavistachurchofchrist.org)*

# <u>WEEK 7</u>

### From the Scriptures

*And all the congregation worshipped, and the singers sang, and the trumpeters sounded, and all this continued until the burnt offering was finished. ~ 2 Chronicles 29:28*

This scripture verse provides an AMAZING visual! I can easily envision this ancient scenario, as if I were a participant in this grand worship experience! Every one of my senses could join in this time of intense worship.

I could *hear* the singers and the trumpets blow harmoniously. I could *see* the congregants lifting and waving their hands. I could *smell* the stifling scent of the sacrificial offering. I could actually *touch* God in this glorious moment. I could *taste* joy! This is a remarkable visual of corporate worship! I can just see and hear this cacophony of sounds erupting from multiple sources within the holy temple. I can envision myself being among this ancient throng, giving it up to God with reckless abandon, all the while the burnt sacrifice is being offered and consumed.

God gets a double dose of pure, undiluted worship. Surely, the assembly must have reveled in such an authentic display of worship. I believe that each time we gather for worship – no matter where it may be - our assemblage ought to pay exclusive reverence and devotion to our Creator. Yet and still, the music alone is not worship; your heart must join in to make the proper melody unto the Lord.

*(All photos: Thinkstock.com)*

# WEEK 8

### From the Scriptures

*"For you shall worship no other god, for the Lord, whose name is Jealous, is a jealous God."*
*~ Exodus 34:14*

This is a commandment from GOD as to preferential treatment towards *Himself.* He makes it clear that one of His many character traits is jealousy. God boldly admits to this, as only He can. GOD even goes so far as to name Himself the very attribute that He has described. All other idols which may have our affection and attention comparable to what He demands, must be resigned… lest we incur His wrath.

   This verse compels me to examine my life to see what or who it is that gets more attention from me than God does. Time to set the record straight, get and KEEP my priorities, affections, and allegiances in proper perspective.

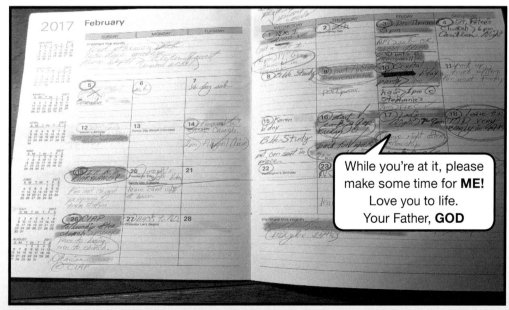

*(Photo: personal collection of Phyllis Hilliard)*

# WEEK 9

### From the Scriptures

*"God is Spirit and those who worship Him must worship in spirit and truth." ~ John 4:24*

This verse is a small extraction from a conversation between Jesus and an anonymous woman from Samaria whom He met at what was known to be Jacob's well. Their conversation went from the subject of satisfying human thirst (or so she thought) to talking about her marital status, to a full discourse on worship. Her identifying Jesus as a Jewish man had little or nothing to do with her former husbands and certainly not the well water, for which she came to draw each day.

This verse focuses on worship being done in a manner akin to the nature, conscience, and embodiment of God. The woman brought up the subject of worship in a slightly controversial tone. Jesus settled the issue by informing her just how worship ought to be done, not so much *where*. The mountain, the well, nor the location has anything to do with worship. Only Spirit and Truth are major players on the court, right along with God.

*(Sketch source: iStock.com)*

# **WEEK 10**

### From the scriptures

*"But if anyone is a worshipper of God and does His will, He hears Him." ~ John 9:31*

Another blind man's sight was restored at the hands and mercy of Jesus. However, this miracle was a questionable event and came under the scrutiny of an influential religious sect, the Pharisees. This sightless man had now been socially empowered. Armed now with a brand new lease on life, he rose to the occasion and boldly challenged the indictments of the Pharisees. Whether through teachings or observances, this man was keenly aware of how God operates. He knew he was a worshipper and that God had heard his prayers to restore or grant him sight. Healing was on the cusp of his deliverance, so long as he fulfilled the will of God.

This verse has taught me that worship - coupled with attending to the will of God - evokes a response *from* God. Keep in mind: although He does hear the cries and prayers of His people, God may not grant our preferred and anticipated answer. Nevertheless, we are obligated to worship Him… in spirit and in truth! (And it won't hurt to add belief in the mix).

*(Sketch source: iStock.com)*

# **WEEK 11**

### From the scriptures

*"Oh come, let us worship and bow down.*
*Let us kneel before the Lord our Maker." ~ Psalm 95:6*

Kneeling and bowing are the ultimate postures for worship, for they beckon us to a place of humility, submission, and as the late Andrew Murray titled one of his books, *Absolute Surrender.* There have been innumerable times throughout my life where I have bowed down and knelt in God's presence. I have prayed fervently, asking God for this and that, pleading with Him to intercept and intercede in my behalf or in behalf of a loved one. I have bowed my head in reverent prayer seeking the face of God to alter what may have appeared to have a disastrous end. I have come to the place of resolve that no matter what goes down, God is sovereign. Nothing – absolutely nothing - changes Who He is.

This verse catapults me to a place of heeding the psalmist and joining in with those who know, who love, who fear, and are awed by God.

*(Photo source: Thinkstock.com)*

# **WEEK 12**

### From the scriptures
*"Worship the Lord in the beauty of holiness."*
*~ Psalm 29:2ᵇ <u>and</u> 1 Chronicles 16:29ᶜ*

I have deeply loved this verse since I first happened upon it nearly 40 years ago when I became a Christian. This entire verse in both Old Testament books is a directive to all who are familiar with the benevolence of God to acknowledge Him. I see worship as the outcome of this reality. Worship is the activity by which we ought to approach God. Holiness is the vehicle – the means –the "how" for entering into this sacred realm.

The psalmist appropriately describes holiness as being 'beautiful.' This is more than being in the eye of the beholder; it is emphatically and indisputably SO. It is not the visible appearance, nor texture of holiness. Holiness is an experience with God which invites us to worship. It is the station, the depot, if you will, where we park ourselves, incline our hearts, tune in and worship.

Beautiful!

*(Photo source: Thinkstock.com)*

# <u>WEEK 13</u>

### From the scriptures

"Then Jehoshaphat stood up in the assembly of Judah and Jerusalem at the temple of the Lord in the front of the new courtyard and said, *'Lord, the God of our ancestors, are you not the God who is in heaven? You rule over all the kingdoms of the nations. Power and might are in your hand, and no one can withstand you.'"*
*~ 2 Chronicles 20:18 (New International Version)*

Just prior to preparing to go into battle, a Levite named Jehaziel told the citizens of Judah and their appointed King Jehoshaphat **not** to fear the opposition but to trust God, in facing the attack of a pursuing enemy. The king gets the message and instead of flexing his political muscle, submitted to the wise counsel of a subordinate. What genuinely reached me with this verse is the fact that Jehoshaphat led the people **by example**. The people in both major regions followed his lead, which culminated in a colossal display of community worship that truncated the efforts of the enemy.

The radical effect of worship is an infusion of unlimited spiritual authority; it is a formidable power source!

**Then**       **Now**

*(Photo source: Thinkstock.com)*

**LEAD BY EXAMPLE**

# <u>WEEK 14</u>

### From the scriptures

*"Now we know that God does not hear sinners, but if anyone is a worshipper of God and does His will, He hears him." ~ John 9:31*

These are the words of a man who was actually defending the fact that God – through Jesus - had restored his sight. The opposing group, also known as Pharisees, vehemently doubted that this man was ever blind at all, that his healing was authentic, or that either could be evidence of the miracles of Jesus. He had concluded that this man, Jesus, indeed worshipped God, otherwise there would be no power, no evidence of answered prayer.

This verse has prompted me to be much more confident about awaiting the outcome of prayers and petitions. My worship brings me and God closer to one another, disavowing and dismissing all negative energies in my immediate sphere, allowing Him to pay full attention to me. As I worship God, he has no other recourse than to incline His ear to me. This is not to say that my request(s) will be granted, but it does guaranteed that as/when I worship, I will have an audience with my Father. With that noted, it is safe to say that we much prefer a one-on-one, undistracted encounter, particularly since He is admittedly a jealous God.

Bottom line: as we worship, God hears us and He wants it to be all about Him!

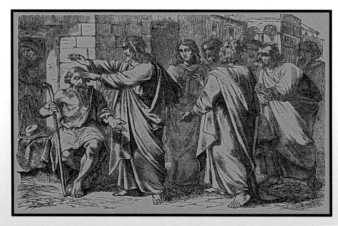

*(Sketch source: iStock.com)*

# WEEK 15

### From the scriptures

*"So all the assembly worshipped, the singers sang and the trumpeters sounded;*
*all this continued until the burnt offering was finished." ~ 2 Chronicles 29:28*

Again, this same scripture referenced earlier in Week 7 is a spectacular rendition of corporate worship! I chose to repeat this because it encompasses the totality and variations of worship. I cannot help but press the point some more. Can't you just see and hear the symphonic sounds erupting from multiple sources within the holy temple? Can't you envision yourself being among this ancient throng described in the scripture, giving it up to God with reckless abandon?

Surely, this ancient assembly must have reveled in such an authentic display of worship. I believe that each time we gather in our temples, churches, synagogues, or wherever we choose to practice our faith, our coming together serves as host to sacred moments of enriched devotion to and fellowship with our Creator, many times accompanied by music.

The worship experience is powerful; it is personal, it is penetrating, it is provocative. Worship is a continuous practice, forging a pronounced alliance between us and God, whose permanence can only be severed by our refusal to surrender and participate.

Ladies and gentlemen, when it comes to keeping your soul in check and worshiping God, may I suggest to you: **BE INTENTIONAL!**

*Photos: Thinkstock.com)*

# END NOTES

## Introduction

[1] Teresa of Ávila was a 16th century Carmelite nun and mystic whose devotion to God was demonstrated through constant prayers and deeds of charity.
For further details, see https://en.wikipedia.org

## Page 21

How Firm A Foundation
Words: R. Keen, rev. The Jubilate group 1982
The Jubilate Group (Admin, Publishing Company, Carol Stream, IL 60188).

Great is Thy Faithfulness
Words: Thomas O. Chisholm, Music: William H. Runyan, 1923
Rev. 1951 Hope Publishing Company, Carol Stream, IL 60188
www.hopepublishing.com.

## Page 34

Matthew 27:5 (New King James Version)

Chapter 1
1. Job 1:13-20
2. II Samuel 12:15-18

Chapter 3
1. http://washingtonmonthly.com/2016/06/06/muhammad-ali-i-am-america
2. How Great Thou Art
Words: Stuart K. Hine,
Music: Swedish folk melody/adapted & arranged: Stuart K. Hine, 1949
1953 The Stuart Hine Trust, CIO, Hope Publishing Co.

Chapter 4

1. *(Webster's Encyclopedic Unabridged Dictionary of the English Language, s.v. "sabbatical")*
2. Mark 6:31
3. Wayne Cordeiro, *Leading on Empty: Refilling your Tank and renewing your passion,* (Bloomington, MN: Bethany House Publishers, 2009), 53.

Chapter 5

1 *(Webster's, s.v. "humility")*
2) *(Webster's, s.v. "mortification)*
3) Matthew 6:3
4) Luke 7:37, 38
5) J.B. Jackson, *A Dictionary of Scripture Proper Names*, (Neptune, NJ: Loizeaux Brothers, 1909, 3rd ed.1957), 50. Jehovah Jireh means God, [my] Provider.

**Jot down a few notes on your personal worship experience.**

_____

_____

_____

_____

_____

_____

_____

_____

_____

_____

_____

_____

_____

_____

_____

_____

*Jot down a few notes on your personal worship experience.*

_____

_____

_____

_____

_____

_____

_____

_____

_____

_____

_____

_____

_____

_____

_____

_____

_____

_____

_____

*Jot down a few notes on your personal worship experience.*

_____

_____

_____

_____

_____

_____

_____

_____

_____

_____

_____

_____

_____

_____

_____

_____

_____

_____

*Jot down a few notes on your personal worship experience.*

**Jot down a few notes on your personal worship experience.**

_____

_____

_____

_____

_____

_____

_____

_____

_____

_____

_____

_____

_____

_____

_____

_____

_____

_____

Printed in the United States
By Bookmasters